MELANCHOLY MUSINGS OF A

SHAMELESS ROMANTIC

Melancholy Musings of a Shameless Romantic

poems by
Karissa Strain

Melancholy Musings of a Shameless Romantic
Copyright © 2024 by Karissa Strain.

All rights reserved. This book or any portion thereof may not be reproduced or used in any manner whatsoever without the express written permission of the author except for the use of brief quotations in the context of reviews.

ISBN: 978-1-0689109-0-6

Cover illustration by Karissa Strain.
Cover design by Rachel Clift.
Book design & layout by Rachel Clift.
rcliftpoetry.com

First printing edition, 2024.

@sistersstrain
sistersstrain.com
The Sisters Strain

The day I met Art is the day I truly became an artist

My poems, my prose, knew no purpose until you injected passion into my pen

CONTENTS

Chapter One
THE LOVER
1

Chapter Two
THE LION
53

Chapter Three
THE LYRICIST
101

Chapter Four
THE LACONIC
183

THE LOVER

Karissa Strain

Maybe a long-ago time
at a different pace
We were Hollywood stars
at the height of our days
If you're Gregory Peck
then could I be your Audrey
We could escape all the crazy
to our own
Roman Holiday

Melancholy Musings of a Shameless Romantic

What if I was Elizabeth Taylor
and you were James Dean
Living a classic film love
straight out of our dreams
Our hearts so Giant
they nearly beat through the screen
Potentials cut short
due to circumstances
unforeseen

Perhaps you're the Rhett Butler
to my Scarlett O' Hara
Like Gone With the Wind
but with a lot less trauma
The ups and the downs
how they pull on the heart strings
Less fear and more love
would have simplified
a lot of things

Could we have a Wonderful Life
if I lassoed you the moon
Like James Stuart
and Donna Reid tried to do
If I couldn't fetch it
I promise I'd try
Anything I could do
to catch your
eye

We might have been Bogart and Bergman
in the Casablanca tale
As Time Goes By
true love would prevail
I'd like to think I'd stay
and wouldn't get on that plane
but love is strange
and shows in
unexpected ways

You've got the style
you dress for the part
Your chivalrous gestures
work their whiles on my heart
I'd wear the dresses; I'd strive to walk with grace
The curled hair
the red lips
the garters
with lace

Karissa Strain

But maybe for right now
we could just be friends
We don't have to be our most classy
or act out pretend
Life isn't a fairy tale
and is hardly ever perfect
Taking a chance on true romance
I'll always deem
worth it

Our souls must meet in our dreams
Bridging the gap between the distance
our physical bodies must daily endure

For no matter how far apart we remain
I still somehow feel fully connected

Karissa Strain

Skinny dipping
has always been
my favorite thing to do

The blanket of stars
shine so bright
the Ocean a deep, dark hue

You joined me
in the water
and our bodies stuck like glue

Basking in
the ambiance
of the mesmerizing moon

It was in
this very moment
my heart got caught in a love

~monsoon~

Melancholy Musings of a Shameless Romantic

You make me feel
like Romeo
and Juliet

All I have are words
and I've already
placed my bet

How can I seem so sure
5 years
since we first met

We're not face to face
but I know I'm going
to love you yet

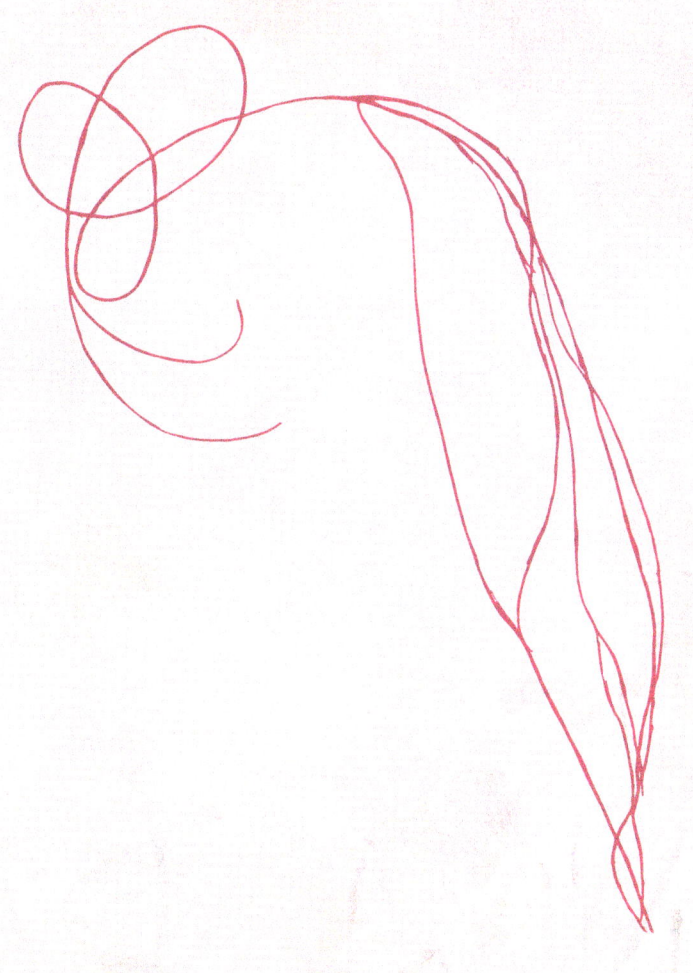

Melancholy Musings of a Shameless Romantic

All I really want to do
    is brush my teeth each night
        right next to you...

    You'll make me laugh
    as your mouth foams
    I'll feel the power
    of being your home
    Darling,
    my love could fill a tome
    This heart of mine
        will never roam

Karissa Strain

 because I know
   that every night
   You'll be the one
   holding me tight
   So babe,
   turn out the light
   Climb into our bed
   kiss me goodnight

 ...This truth of mine shall never sway
   This forever remains
     the best part of my day

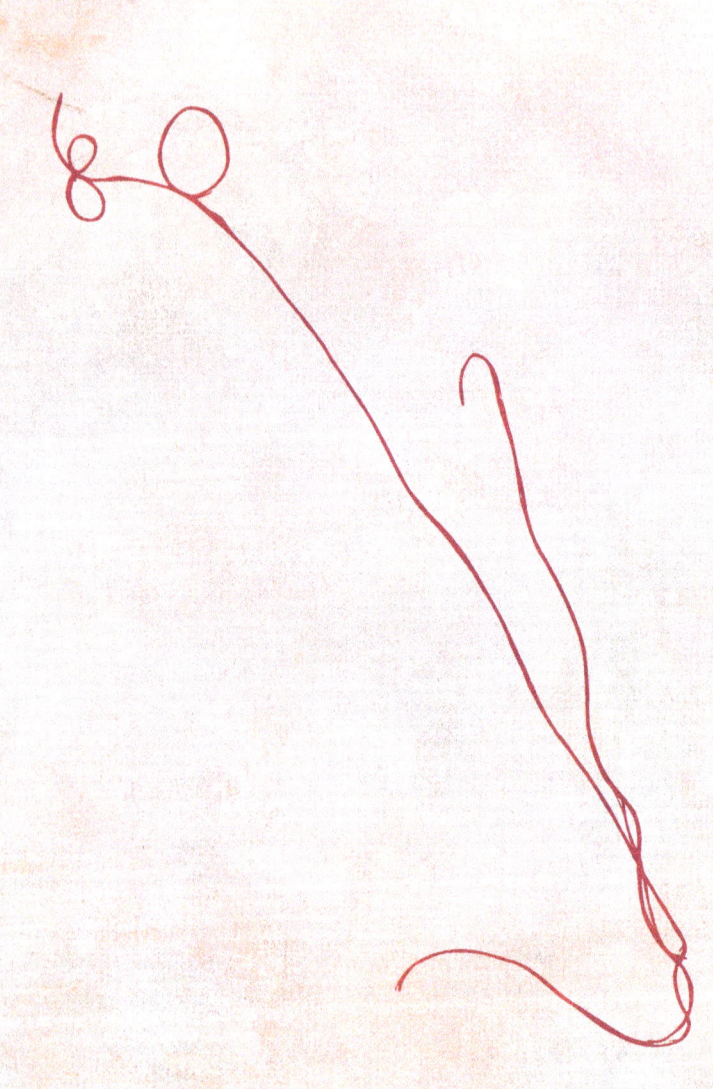

Anchor Me

Karissa Strain

You take me back to the river
Where my heart's never beat quicker...

Unlock parts of me
I hid long ago
The first person I've genuinely
wanted to know
Where my mind goes
as my eyes stare
You stare back and ask
I yearn to dare
It's not that I don't trust
I'm just fucking scared
Never believed
anyone who said they cared
How will I feel
If you don't flow my way
If yours isn't the bank
I'm intended to stay
It seems my hearts
been forever left to roam
But you're the closest
in a long time
that I've felt
to home

...and my hearts never beat quicker
So please, darling, take me back to that river

Melancholy Musings of a Shameless Romantic

You're the tide
flowing in and out
while its steadiness remains

I can be your shore
accepting all your waves
calmly, through life's many banes

Karissa Strain

If you'll be the stars
with their guiding light
in their constant constellations

I'll be the moon
shining bright
with every cycling rotation

Melancholy Musings of a Shameless Romantic

If I knew I couldn't keep you
would I still choose to stay
or should I save myself the heartbreak
get out now, push you away

I say I'm open minded
not black or white, I'm grey
but my feelings aren't so clouded
I fear they won't easily stray

I would be broken hearted
if this wasn't true
I'm scared no one else
could ever live up to you

You make loving easy
when all I've ever known is hard
For the first time in my life
I'm not hiding any cards

Whirling Whimsy

Melancholy Musings of a Shameless Romantic

I fell asleep late last night
thinking of you
Wondering if you realize how enamored I am
with all that you do
Your passion, your talent
the true expression of your art
The way your face shines pure kindness
the depth and honesty of your heart

You are thought of by me every single day
I don't always know what it is I should say
I want to know how you are doing, if you're feeling okay
but worry my questions might push you farther away
I wish there was something more I could do
to make you feel as cherished and appreciated as you deserve to
So much love exists inside of you
One of the most beautiful souls I ever knew
I'm here for you for anything you need
For a talk, a hug, or company
I'm always only a text or phone call away
I'll get on that train to get to you any time of day
If you have no words that you feel you can say
but want a warm body beside you, I would quietly stay
And if you don't want company I'll understand
Just know that I am here with an outstretched hand
We've been spending time apart, but my thoughts are never far
Even if you feel you can't see me, I'll keep loving you on par

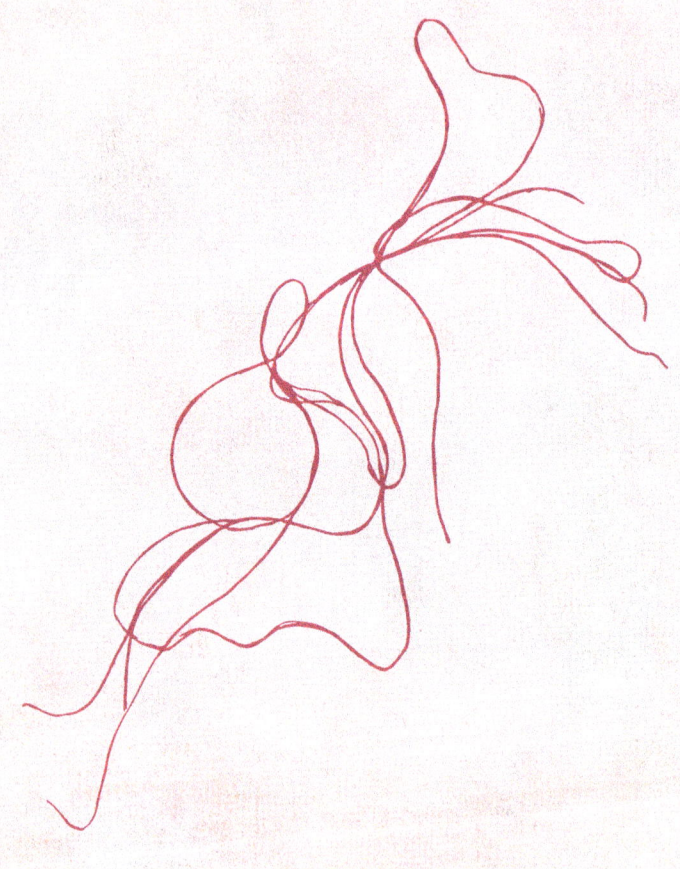

Bus Ride

Karissa Strain

Our souls
can travel to places
of which
our bodies
can only wish
to be

~Let them be free to roam~

Melancholy Musings of a Shameless Romantic

Happiness is...

Heartbreak is...

Happiness is knowing the incarnation of the man
I have always dreamed of exists in you

    Heartbreak is brought on by the longing of which
    the distance between us taunts me regularly

Happiness is knowing there is another human in the world
who I seem to resonate with at such ease
bringing me feelings of comfort and "home"

> Heartbreak can only be known
> through the tragedy of witnessing a beautifully sad love story
> for our "homes" are in different countries

Happiness because I am not the only soul
that views the essence of love
in such high regard

    Heartbreak because knowing love that fierce and honest
    does exist and is possible to experience
    breaks my heart in and of itself

Melancholy Musings of a Shameless Romantic

You're the love I always wanted
but didn't think exists
I was shocked when I found you
my mind filled with bliss
How is it fair
separated by such distance
Your love is a treasure
I don't have
for which

~I wish~

Karissa Strain

Like the Earth to the moon
you're what I need
Through the passing of time
and all possible creed
Your gravitational pull
slows my speed
You'll always see
the same side of me

I missed you way before I left you

I missed you even before I met you

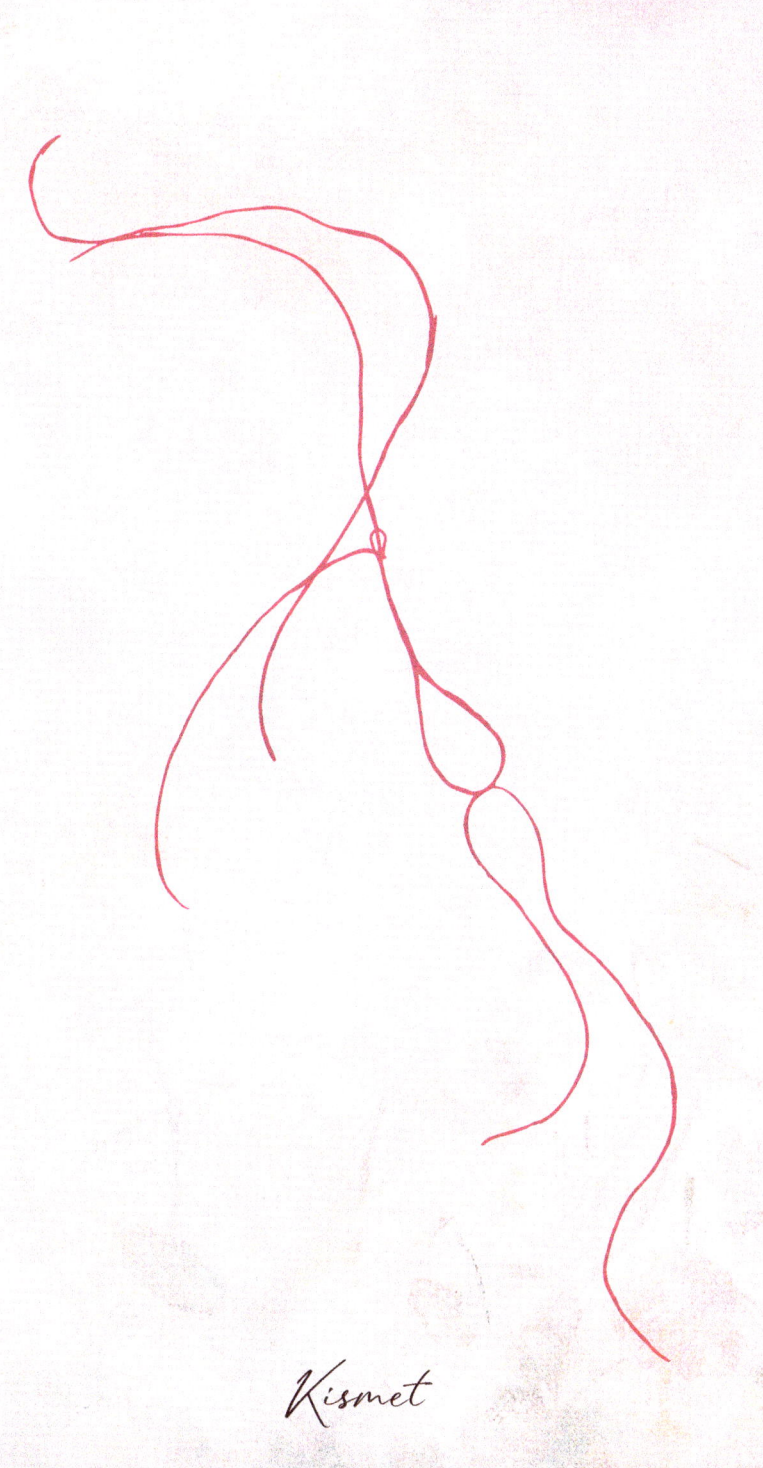

Melancholy Musings of a Shameless Romantic

I can feel myself falling
Not in the way I have fallen before
They say leap and the net will appear
Well I'm sunk into your mesh
Body weightless
Heart racing from the release
Never been so afraid
Excitement courses through my veins
I could do it
Really do it this time
I could let myself fall
Shed the skin of my past fool
and finally be seen as I am
No barrier
No protection
Real, honest, naked
Your lips hardly graze me
and I want to jump all over again
I want to jump every day
and every day
I want to be caught
by you

If I was to write you a love letter
I'd tell you you're the most beautiful contradiction
I've ever witnessed
I adore how deep and poignant your soul resonates
Yet you never cease to bring forth a light-hearted humor
I recognize it as being akin to my own
and it makes me hopeful my romantic soul
has finally found its

~home~

Grand Gesture

Karissa Strain

You're the warm crackling fire
on a cold winter's night
You're the soft, cool breeze
in the dead of summer's plight
You're the bright blossoming flowers
that from the rains grew
You're the leaves changing and falling
with a promise to renew
You're everything to me
My heart forever

~belongs to you~

Finding myself
feeling kind of lost
My love runs fierce
but at what cost
Never been good
at keeping my cool
Always destined to play
the lovestruck fool

Karissa Strain

There's no greater love
to fill your body
then when you love yourself
Drink in the life bearing water
quench your thirst and health
Breathe into every inch
of your being
Fill that empty shell
Feel the energy that is flowing
push forward

~develop~

She may have your presence
but I feel I have your soul
It visits me in vivid dreams
and holds me while I weep
It's a ghost that stays
close in my chest
It calms and comforts me
through the days of living without you
I wonder if I'm a ghost
in your chest too

Do I bring you any comfort?

Melancholy Musings of a Shameless Romantic

I crave you everyday...

> I crave your intellect
> I crave your art
> I crave your intelligence
> Want to overwhelm your heart
>
>> I crave your humor
>> I crave your goals
>> I crave your affections
>> Want to resonate in your soul

I want to trace the freckles on your back
to a map that leads me home

I need to know if it is safe there
or if I should continue to roam

Your blue eyes shone like the northern star
guiding me when I felt alone

The strength of your body, the warmth of your arms
provide a security I've never known

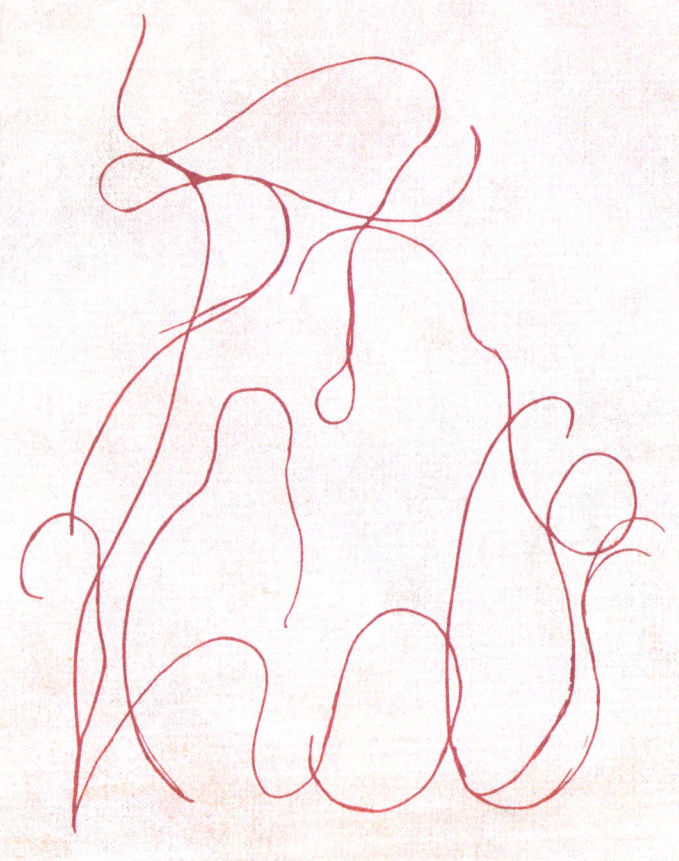

Evening Gown

There's a dress
in my wardrobe
I save just for you
It's a
sort of periwinkle
purply/blue
The first time
I wore it
was a day spent, us two
The day I really knew
the love I felt for you
was

~ true ~

The Ocean reminds me too much of you
I feel the soft caress of your skin
in the image of it's endless blue
It's always been the visual of my dreams
and that still remains true
I see the pale sky touch it's dark depths
and I wish it was a representation of us two

Sunday evenings seem to be
when I sense you the most
I wonder if it's because somewhere out there
you are thinking of me as strongly as I am of you
I like to believe that maybe our souls
meet in our dreams on Sunday nights
Maybe that would explain
why I wake up every Monday
missing you with a renewed fierceness
Our souls know we should be together
and they are brave enough
to cross the boundaries
that we are not

Melancholy Musings of a Shameless Romantic

Always been looking for that easy love
the kind that feels just right

Missing the way you held me close
all through the long, dark night

We said we weren't, but it felt like were
and for a chance I was willing to fight

But I need a man who inspires me
and will lift me up with their light

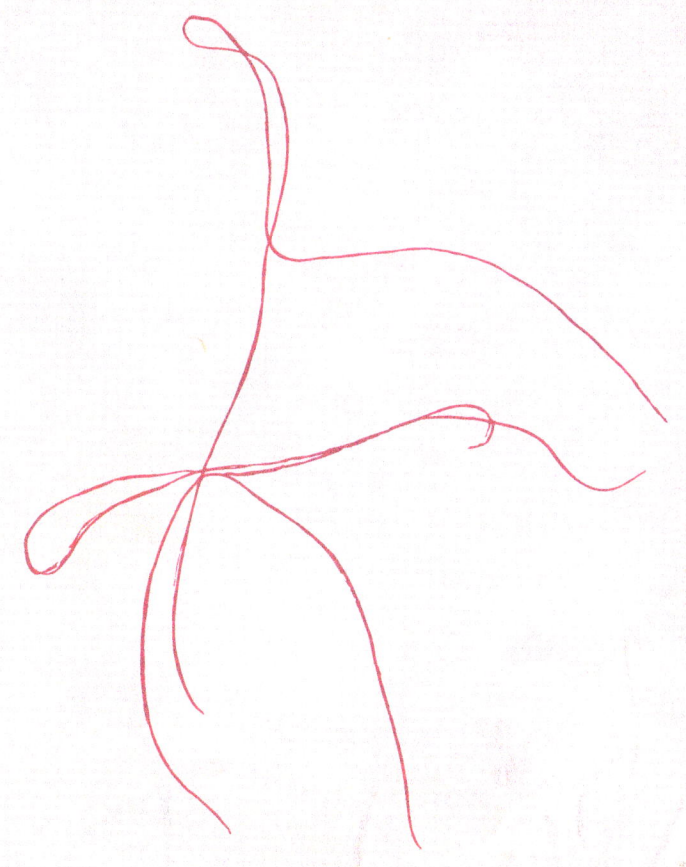

Big Dip-her

Melancholy Musings of a Shameless Romantic

Most days I feel the strongest longing to be home
It's been a long time since I remember feeling anything close to it
In fact, I don't know that I've ever truly been there
Yet some how I feel I know what it is-what it could be
It isn't a city or a country or a house with four walls and a roof
Home, I believe, is found within a person
A person I feel safe and comfortable with
Home is understanding and openness and vulnerability
Something that can be built stronger over time

Will I ever feel at home, I often wonder?
Would I recognize it if I found it?
Does it even exist?
Or is it a figment of my romantic mind...a dream I have curated
which will never be attainable?

Because for a long while now, my love's been lost
and I fear it may never be found

THE LION

Karissa Strain

It was tragic when we met
that we lived so far apart
Tragic I barely knew you
but you somehow stole my heart
Tragic you became the inspiration
behind every piece of my art
Tragic we now live in the same town
but our lives remain apart

Melancholy Musings of a Shameless Romantic

It is tragic I still have feelings
and must keep them to myself
Tragic I must bottle you
and put you on the shelf
It was tragic you chose someone else
you did what you had to do
But the tragedy for me
is that I'm still in love with you

Karissa Strain

It was tragic I could picture
exactly what our lives could be
Tragic I saw my future
and you were there alongside me
Tragic for the first time
I felt I had found my home
Tragic you pulled away
and now my hearts been left to roam

Tragic I wasn't ready
for you to be out of my life
Tragic I felt the longing
of one day becoming your wife
Tragic I find it hard to date
the comparisons are too few
Yeah, the tragedy for me
is that no one equals you

Karissa Strain

Nothing pulls me farther
from the love
I found in you
Then knowing the sparks
that sprang
between us once
have now become moot
What is there
for me to do
to bring it back to life
'cause all I dream of lately
is becoming your

~wife~

Melancholy Musings of a Shameless Romantic

I know what I want
I know what's my truth
Baby it's up to you

I don't know
what's going on in your mind
but you don't call me lover

~anymore~

Push & Pull

Melancholy Musings of a Shameless Romantic

I feel him fading
in communication and contact
but in spirit
I always feel him
so strongly

~it brings me to tears~

Karissa Strain

We came this far
I didn't get here myself
It seems to me
you put our love on the shelf
Don't leave me here
feeling all alone
So much potential
we've got left to hone

Melancholy Musings of a Shameless Romantic

I can't turn you off
I can't shut you out
Never been good
at distancing myself
From what it is
that my heart feels
Got no compartments
to help me heal

Karissa Strain

How do you do it
Show me your ways
To turn off our love
and go about your days
I want to understand
Baby, tell me, what's your plan?
Will we ever be together?
or is this storm going to

~weather us~

Speechless.
That's the way you leave me
When you've got nothing more to say to me
Both of us just
Speechless.

Karissa Strain

Fear is a bitch.

I'm afraid of going
but I'm also afraid I'll never go

I'm afraid of letting myself fall in love
and yet I'm scared to death of never loving

Either way,
fear remains the only guarantee

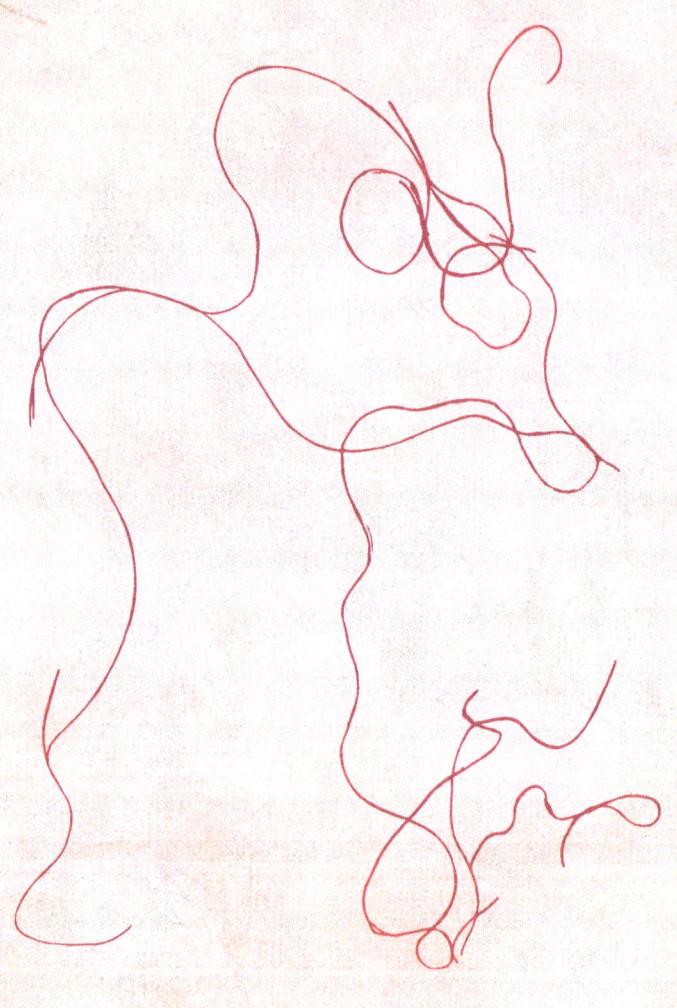

Nimble Nightmare

Karissa Strain

Can't breathe
Can't catch my breath
Little bits fall apart
Slowly melt away from me
Sliding on a tear
they leave me
I wallow in the thought
The mind it races

Pictures.

Words.

Remembrances.

Melancholy Musings of a Shameless Romantic

Gone for good
or just put on pause
How do I fight
when I don't know the cause
What will it be
at the end of the day
The love
it falters
then falls

~away~

Karissa Strain

Seems so far but held so dear to my heart
It hurts
The remedy unclear

Melancholy Musings of a Shameless Romantic

The longing
The lust-
How to turn it off
When the subject disappears
and you're left with just dust
It doesn't fade
It won't let you steer
It has such control
You can't just press

~clear~

Karissa Strain

Is it ever okay to love with such force
If I had the chance
would I choose a new course

Without you I can't hear the music
and that terrifies me
This silence has me suffocating
I can hardly breathe

My heart

It falls to pieces
Your love the only glue
To put me back together
Make me whole and new

Soul Meets Body

Deep inside
The heart it stirs
Like a thousand
Swarming bees
It's intense
It stings
It's fierce enough
To knock you
To your knees
Once you taste
The nectar
You know
Nothing else
Will please
So be the Queen
Rule your colony
To garner
Your treasured

~honey~

I never meant to make you feel worse
by making myself feel better
Your comfort fit me
like a flannel sweater
I thought it was mutual
it was a give and take
My intentions were real
they were never once fake
I'm sorry you're hurting
I can't take it back
Can't be what you wanted
but for love, there's no lack
I'll be a pillar
I can weather the storm
So let your winds rage
until you feel norm-al
again

I don't want
the ones that want me
Their love is false
unreal, fleeting
But the ones I want
never seem to want me back
What do I choose
when the options are stacked

~against me~

This is the portrait of a woman
When she is happy
she smiles
It lights up the room
and lasts for a while
But sometimes it fades
Her demeanor turns gray
The smile gets lost
Why? She'll never say

Just know that she's okay

Because love, like life
is hardly black and white
It's those in between grays
that make it worthy
of our fight
No life isn't about living
for unattainable glories
They say everyone is evil
in somebody's story

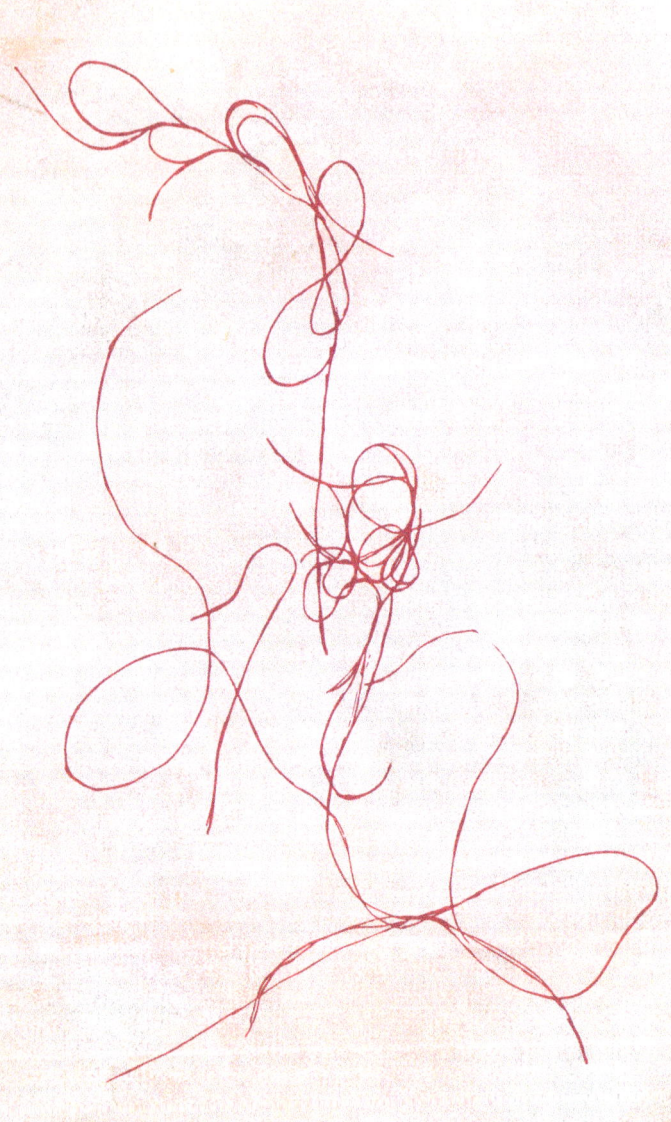

Balancing Act

Karissa Strain

I hate that you are a coward
I hate that you settled for the safe choice
I hate that you didn't feel safest with me

But I feel sorry for the woman you're with
when you can't seem to set me free

The explanations
To justify
The weight of it all
Tears me up inside
Should be short
Complete
Succinct
But that's just simply
Not how I think
I'm the girl
Who always says too much
Feels it all
With the bad, bad luck
Gotta get it out
Gotta say it all
Can't leave these words
Resting on

~my heart~

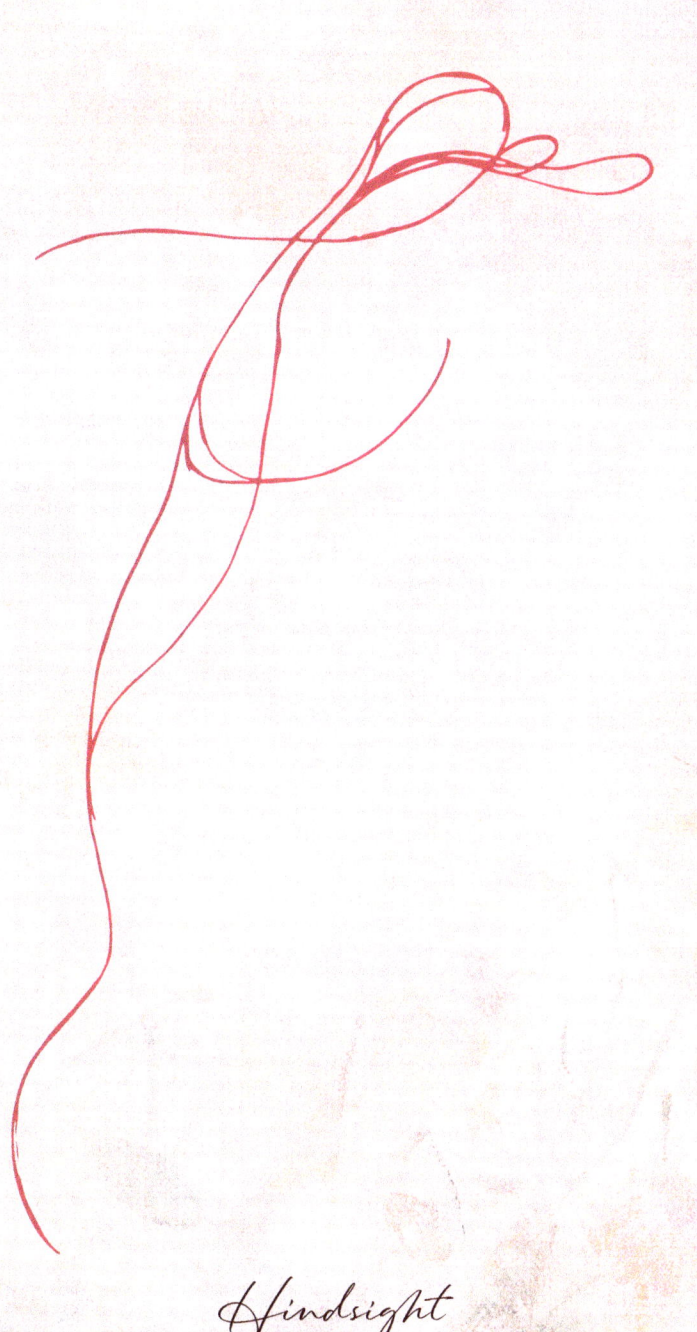

Hindsight

I miss your darkness
I miss your depth
I miss holding your hand
As we'd walk together in step
I miss your charming smile
I miss your pretty eyes
I miss how much ketchup was required
Whenever the two of us ate fries
I miss making you pancakes
I miss getting you ice cream from sprouts
I miss you sending me selfies
With the most adorable fucking pout
I miss you saying you miss me
I miss calling you love
I miss your arms wrapped around me
God, I'd kill to embrace you in a hug
I miss sharing margaritas
I miss make-outs at Harvard and Stone
I miss being yours
My heart, from you, refuses to roam
But I think this is temporary
You never fit me like a glove
It's just fond memories I miss
You and I were never really in love

Karissa Strain

I don't trust myself after you
Maybe I had unrealistic expectations of what love is
Maybe everything I felt was right
but it just wasn't right for us
But how do I live with that now?
Will time whittle away those feelings to a point
where I realize they were just lust?
Do I hold out for something
that matches/tops those feeling?
You've taken away my confidence
You've made me question those gut feelings
that came so strongly with you
I could see my future, I could see it clearly
I could see it with you and how well you fit me
Now I feel like I'm an unsure traveller
who has lost their shoes along the way
and that holds them back from exploring every terrain
Trying to learn how to feel their way again
but feeling far too cautious about stubbing a toe
or stepping on broken glass

Inspire me
Ignite my soul
Start a fire
in me
'Cause my fuse
is short
I'm ready
to

~burn~

Karissa Strain

I can feel the tide of his emotions
ebbing and flowing

I know when he is available
and when he has checked out

It turns my insides wild

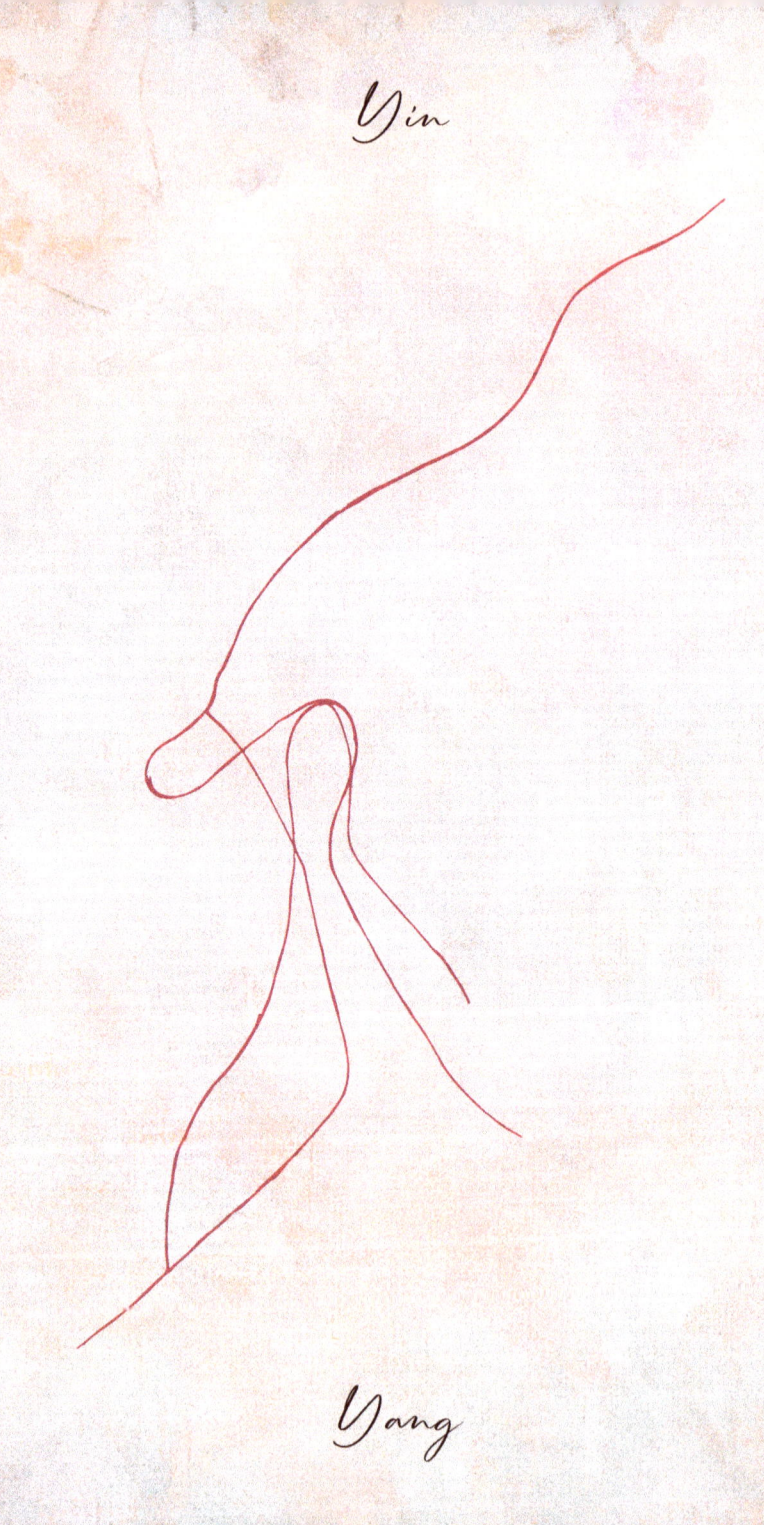

Karissa Strain

Collecting lovers
Like sand dollars in the ocean
Don't be fooled by their name
It's only sentimental notion

Dollars with untradeable currency
A value not intended to be monetary
Worth their weight in experience alone
But not everyone, we bring with us home

They're not a dollar and they'll never be

No matter how much it seems their truth rings
The color, the texture, or nostalgia they bring
They'll never amount
To the real thing

Like the tide flows in and out
Touching upon the sandy bank
Parts of them remain with me
And parts of me with them
I await another tide to come
And bring a new sand dollar in

Bereft Butterfly

Melancholy Musings of a Shameless Romantic

Nothing cuts harsher
then a love unadorned
My heart stays open
but my soul is scorned
Every day the dagger inches deeper
Drawing a wedge
in my sensitive demeanor

Karissa Strain

Every time I think I'm close
I get pulled back down again

Reality is a fickle bitch
and she is not my friend

The world classifies you
Labels you
Puts you in a box
Six full sides
You can't get out of
No matter
how hard
you

~knock~

Karissa Strain

I wanna be
the tree
at the edge of the island
So close
the water
touches my skin
Leaning
so far
I fear I'll fall in

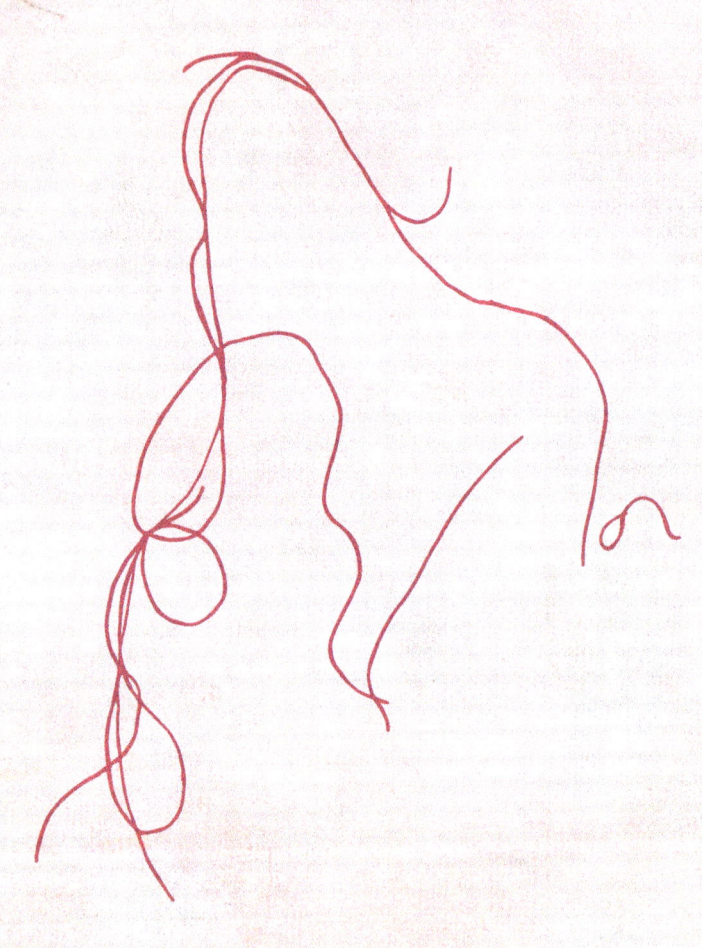

Half-mast

"I want to make you so fucking happy"
You whispered in my ear passionately
In the outfit that you bought me
Those words are going to haunt me

"I could see myself falling madly in love with you"
The first time our bodies became one, no longer two
You touched me like you knew exactly what to do
I wondered if those words were genuinely true

"I love you baby" you whispered three times
I asked if you meant it and looked you in the eyes
We both know you said it, that you can't deny
It's the intention behind it that became the lie

"Stay with me, I miss you when you go"
It was too soon to move in, that we both know
Your emotional retraction hit me with a hard blow
I guess it's a connection no longer meant to grow

"That's your decision" and you let me off the hook
It was a short affair, but it still has me shook
It seems I was the wrong girl who just had the right look
So I'll be the scapegoat, I'll play it by the book

"I'll take myself out of the equation"
Maybe the ghost of someone else, on your mind,
makes frequent invasions
I'll let go of the hard feelings, I'm sure it wasn't your intention
I just hope you're mindful, in the future,
of your words before they're mentioned

THE LYRICIST

Karissa Strain

Where did you go
when you ran away
Why did you lock your heart
in a dead bolt cage
No way to break in
no way to penetrate
How could we have known
this would be your

~fate~

The Smile you wore
shone so bright
The perfect camouflage
to your private plight
But what could be different
if granted the chance
I hope your spirits coalescing
on life's everlasting

~dance~

Karissa Strain

I wish you knew
how to let your troubles out
I wish you knew
how to face the years of doubt
I wish you knew
how to let your guard down
Most of all
I'm wishing we had more than

~wishes~

I want to be
everything that you need
I want to look into the eyes
of a man who's in love with me
I want to know
in my heart
that this is the one
The one who grounds me
and makes me feel like I am

~home~

Karissa Strain

I know you're my "who"
I know this is true
'Cause I feel all those things
whenever I'm with you
It doesn't have to be hard
It doesn't have to be a tragedy
Just give me your hand now
Darling
take this leap

~with me~

Melancholy Musings of a Shameless Romantic

He says I am the woman of his dreams
I have every intention of making those dreams a reality

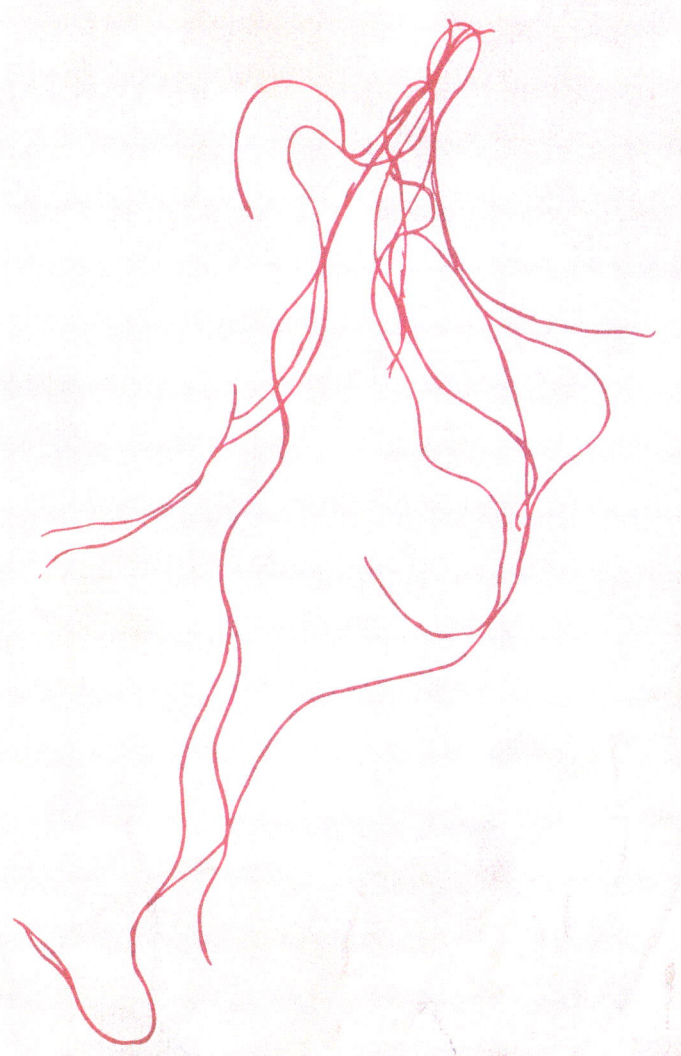

Womanly Waterfalls

Melancholy Musings of a Shameless Romantic

The sky is dark
but the moon is shining through
I'm happy
because I'm there with you
I watch you sleep
with those pouty
baby mouthed lips
Those lips
I long to
kiss

Karissa Strain

Now you are asleep
I imagine I am there
Soft kiss to your cheek
and a stroke of your hair
I can feel you all around me
even though you're far away
We may not be together
but this love
is here
to stay

Melancholy Musings of a Shameless Romantic

We spent the day
in the garden
planting seeds

None of the flowers
ever grew

That's when your love
started sprouting
in my heart

A field
of wild flowers

Karissa Strain

I hear your thoughts
as though you're speaking
next to me

Even though
we're living miles apart

Should weeds start growing
in that field
for all to see

I'll be
your gardener

Love
you know I'm with you
When our hearts
feel black and blue
I know you'll still
come shining through
Even when
it hurts like hell
and our eyes
from tears they swell
I know you'll always find a way
in your arms
to make me

~stay~

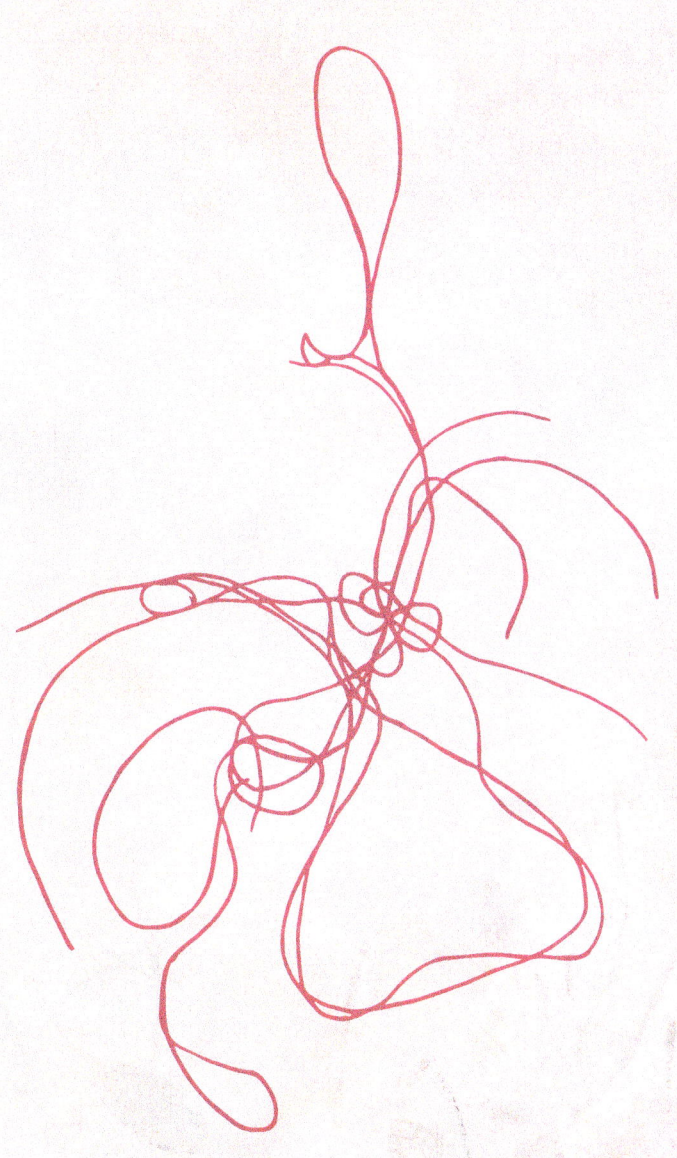

Surrender

They say time is on our side
Gotta take it easy on your pride
Give up the reigns and enjoy the ride
Let the stars be your guide

I guess I'm just hoping
one day

Those stars will lead you back
my way

Karissa Strain

We have a connection
contrived by
the constellations

Take all the time you need
If it's worth having
it's worth waiting for

I'll wait for you
until the stars
coming shining through

When it's our time baby
you best believe
I'll come running to you

I know you gotta go
but I wish you could stay
I don't want to be the one
to have to say
Goodbye

~I don't want to let you go this way~

Karissa Strain

Running, running, running
My heart
it skips a beat
My feet
they keep me moving
but I'm running
out of steam
My hair it billows
in the wind
I feel my hope
is running thin
Sweat drips down
my face
and I'm holding
back

~a scream~

Keep
Keep fighting
My pulse beats
Flash
Like lightning
I'm gonna
Keep
Keep fighting
Breathe
As my chest
Is tightening

Karissa Strain

Stumbling through the bushes
and I'm ready
to attack
My hearts laid out this plan
and I'll follow it
as my map
My bodies aching
as I trip
Scrape my knee
and bruise my shin
There's no will power that I lack

~nothings gonna hold me back~

Melancholy Musings of a Shameless Romantic

You say
you won't go
But I know
you won't stay home
You're waiting
always anticipating
for some better plans
to come along

Karissa Strain

You keep me dangling
on a string
When you want me
always at your whim
Holding the power
with your deck of cards
You know
on my sleeve
is where I keep

~my heart~

I can't keep giving
all of me
To someone who
would rather just be free
If I'm not cool enough
to fit your popularity
Then trust me baby
this ain't where
I want to be

Karissa Strain

One day I'm the one
the next I'm not
You're making my head spin
this feeling
can't be fought
Don't know what I'm doing
or how to get release
You just keep pulling
the rug
from underneath
of me

It ain't nice
to be the lover

Who's always thinking of the other

With no thought given in return

Feel the heart ache as it burns

Don't make me
be the lover

I'll find myself
another

~another lover~

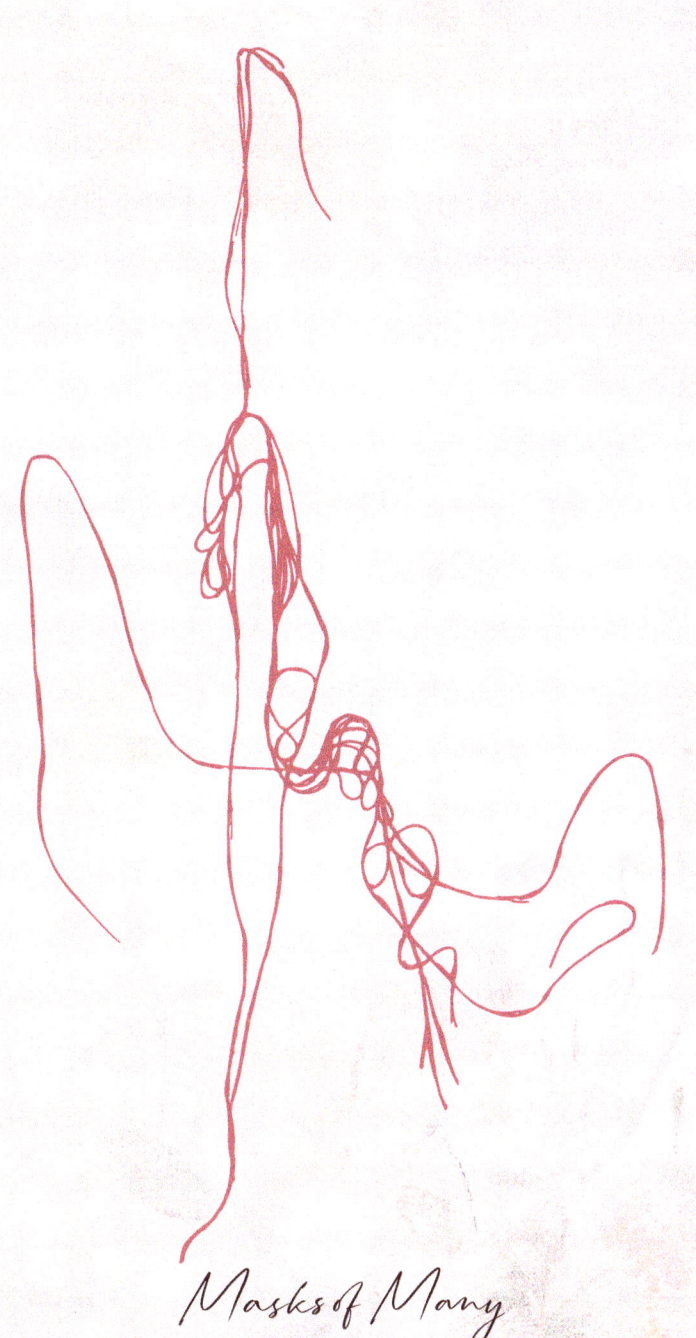

I'll be the needles that knit the yarn
If you'll be the mitts that keep our hands warm

Your camera speeds as fast as my heart
Just one look at me and my mind falls apart

I'll be the jam you spread on your scone
Whatever flavor you crave is the one I'll hone

If you'll be the home I come running to
Every morning I wake it'll be next to you

Melancholy Musings of a Shameless Romantic

I'll be the lyrics to your two-piece band
You stomp your feet and I'll clap my hands

If you'll be the stars then I'll be your moon
You'll always be the endless sky touching my ocean blue

Karissa Strain

Baby
Be my easy
Be my easy love

~Be my easy love~

Melancholy Musings of a Shameless Romantic

I can't believe
how much I've changed
My body was an empty shell
I was buried in a grave
My eyes we're closed
to what the world could be
Focused on the obvious
never searching for more to be seen
If you ask
you never know
what you're going to receive

Karissa Strain

It's never hard
to choose the right path
If your eyes are open to the signs
you'll find the guidance that you lack
You have to learn to trust
in the strength of the unknown
Just because you can't see it
doesn't mean you're on your own
If you try
you never know
the success you could hone

Melancholy Musings of a Shameless Romantic

Like an animal
Feeling out of control
My heart wants more
My instincts are

~taking over~

Karissa Strain

I'm like an animal
Feeling out of control
It's my hearts turn to rule
Gonna let it

~take me over~

Karissa Strain

When you said
I was the woman of your dreams
I asked you if you meant it
You assured me
with a sweet embrace
that you said them 'cause you felt it
Words have never held more weight
then when they rolled off
your loving lips
But I guess the expression is true
Loose lips
really do sink ships

And baby, we were the Titanic

Melancholy Musings of a Shameless Romantic

I wrote you a letter or two
and poured it all out on the page
For I felt ours was
an old-fashioned love
despite our living in a modern age
Each day I hoped a letter you'd return
A year passed
and the longing lasts
The distance never swayed my heart like yours
You put me on pause
and kept me locked
in the past

And baby I thought my Jack was more Rock'n'roll than that

Karissa Strain

You said the rest of the world gets concrete
But I'd always get playdough
So I let myself be breakable
And you handled me
Carelessly

Oh, carelessly
You handled me

~carelessly~

Lately I've been trying
been trying to come back to you
'Cause baby
when you're gone
I'm feeling lonely
and oh so blue
It was never what I wanted
never wanted us to be through
It was just our foolish notions
not our love
that we

~outgrew~

Karissa Strain

To live without you baby
would shatter me in two
My soul forever restless
wandering
in search of you
Don't tell me you've moved on
On to someone new
'Cause you're my one and only
more than my words
it's true

It started here
just like this tonight
You leaned up on the bar
your guys all by your side

I caught your eye
how that made me sigh
A smirk played across your face
and the sparks did fly

You made it hard
for me to perform
I knew not who you were
...but I was craving more

Karissa Strain

You were for me
I was for you
We were happy enough
'till it all came unglued

There was no wrong
No such thing as right
Our love just came and went
...like the old Ocean tide

It's the words that you'd say
In the songs that you once sang

Now their gone, they fade away
Like the birds in a "v"
on a crisp fall day

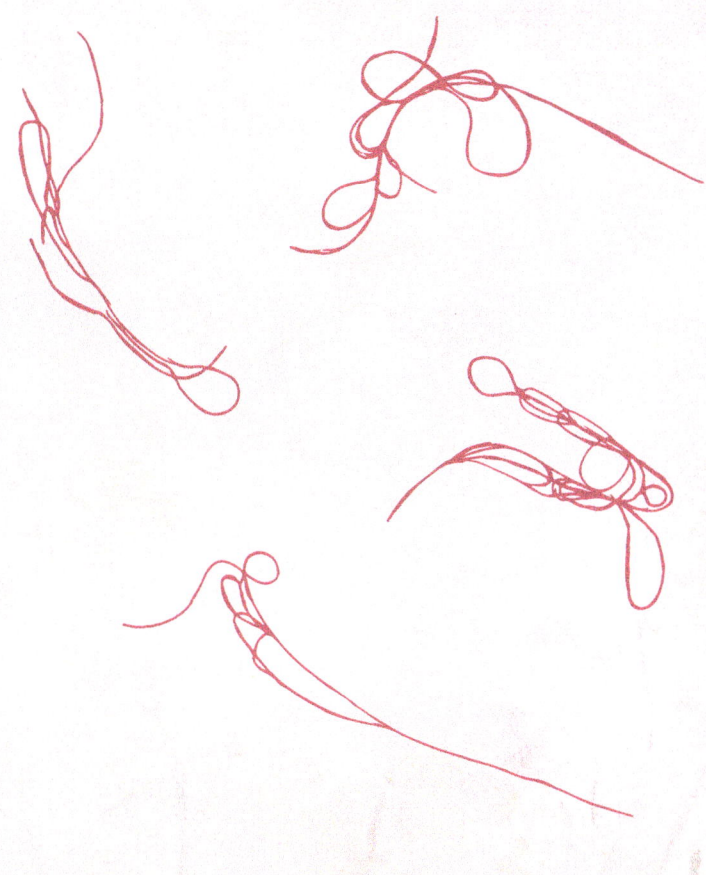

Yearning... Churning

Love
is the hardest
game to play
because there's no guarantees
at the end of the day

Take a chance
with me
let's be free, what do you say
If we fall that's okay
we'll move on in our ways

Karissa Strain

You've left
but never gone
You're always somewhat
on my mind
Be it the lessons
that I've learned
or the nostalgia
marked by
time

I don't hate you
and you don't hate me
Just two strong souls
not meant to be
I'm moving fast
while you're moving slow
We're butting heads
with no where
to go

Karissa Strain

It's okay
we'll both be fine
We'll find other partners
for this ride
I'm wishing you all
the best there is
with one last hug
and goodbye
kiss

...you'll still be missed

This can't be the way
it was meant to be
I'm hoping this life
is only temporary
'Cause the fear inside
strikes a storm in me
Hoping someday soon
I'll be free
From the monetary shackles
that ransack me
Not even sure my heart
is still beating
This desperation
leaves me lost
and grieving

Karissa Strain

This world has taken
all I have to give
Feeling depleted
of my life blood
will to live
Now don't take me at my word
It's just a figure of speech
At the moment my options
are feeling
obsolete

I'm not going to do anything
drastic or dumb
Just this loneliness inside
has got me feeling
sort of numb
Hopin' and dreamin'
for a switch up
a change
Fighting with myself
about playing the game
My sensitivities may make me
appear lame
But they are what keep me
from staying
the same

The more I struggle
the more I grow
The more I feel this
the more I know
There is simply no other
path for me to take
If I have to burn
than leave me on this stake
One things for sure
you'll never find me fake
'Cause this ain't a notion
I'll soon shake
I may be broke
but I'll never be broken
Perpetually
Graciously
I remain hopin'
My heart and soul
will always
be open

Take me as I am
don't ever take me
for granted
This passion is one
that is deeply rooted
and planted
I may not have
all the answers
now
But I know I'll make it
some way
somehow

Karissa Strain

Don't underestimate
the efforts I'll take
Don't underestimate
the sacrifices I'll make
This was in the stars
it's destiny
it's fate
I'll never live a life
out of fear
or hate
That's never been me
that's not what I do
Hoping one day
my words will get through
My path will be aligned
with a cause that's true
Thank you for listening
signed sincerely,

~from me to you~

Melancholy Musings of a Shameless Romantic

So many stars around
Watch them one by one
as their lights
fade out

Twinkling no more
their marks left the sky
One more chance
has died

Karissa Strain

Start to break apart
Leaving me
without a solid
heart

Try to hold them close
Compressing the pieces
ready to
explode

They may not be ready
but here I come
My fire is a burnin'
gonna have some fun
Tired of the hate
now I'm showering love
Gonna meteor
and crash right into this

~world~

Karissa Strain

When
will my time come
I've been reaching for the sun
Every time that I get close
I can feel it burn
Searing at my skin
still my heart it

~yearns~

When
will I make it
Trying so hard not to fake it
Never wanted
anything so bad
Hate that there's something
I can't have

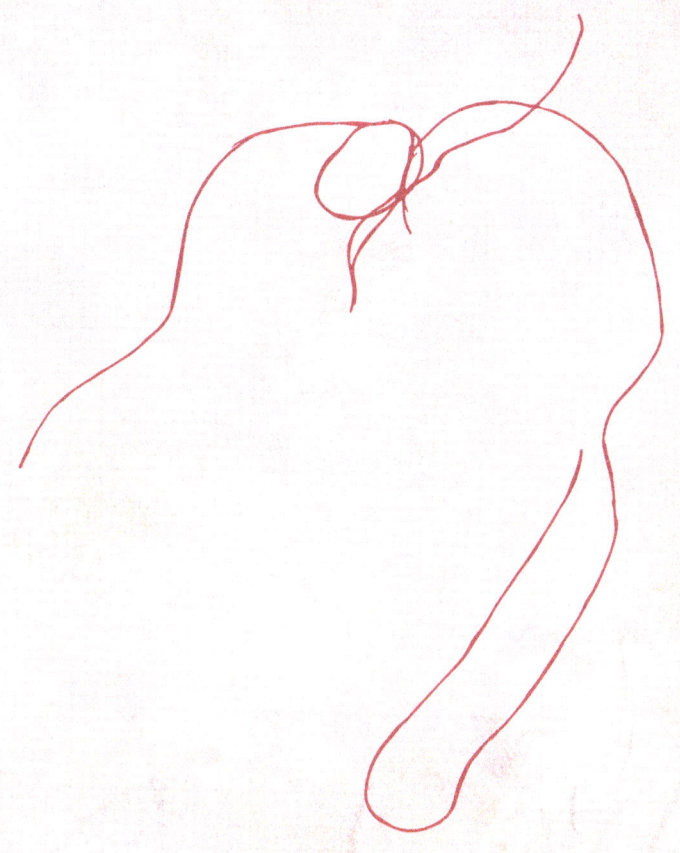

Bent Over Backwards

We don't have to be
anything more than friends
To enjoy the company
of each others
loneliness

It's our hearts that bare the mark
We're both numb and scarred
Let's just put another record on
and sing along
in the dark

We could unite
Maybe spend the night
Dancing in the dark
in the pale moon light
and holding each other tight

I'm not tied to you
and you've no debt to me
Our spirits join together now
but our hearts are
roaming free

There's a coldness all around
it's dark and damp
The light is drowning out
still I feel there's a chance
My breathe it leaves my lips
and floats away
Should no one hear my words
I'll take them to my grave

But this ain't the life
I want to lead
Just want someone
to take a chance on me

Give me time
and I promise
you will see

~shine a light on me~

Karissa Strain

Hope it fills my chest
and overflows
I'm on the right path
and my heart it knows
I can feel it in my soul
as my blood burns red
Surging through my veins
rushing to my head

Come so close
but it's still so far
If this damn breaks
it'll drown my heart

Still I see
there's reason
to believe

~shine a light on me~

Melancholy Musings of a Shameless Romantic

I want
the very best for you
I want you to find a love that's true
Take your time
do it right
Have patience with yourself
don't give up
the fight

I want
you to find what inspires you
what sets your soul on fire and enlivens you
and when you do
never let it go
You only get one chance
to put on the
best show

Karissa Strain

I'm wishing
for you a heart that's full
and a spirit that's light and free
Never lose that kind desire
to follow through on your good deeds
because you're the kind of human
the world truly
needs

I'm wishing
for you the loveliest view
wherever your life's road may lead you to
And if our paths
should ever cross again
I hope you'll recognize me
as a dear old
friend

I know I'm not the woman
whose life will be spent with you
but I've enjoyed every minute of this time
that we've been through

Some loves were meant for seasons
Some loves were meant for years
Some loves bring you lessons
and with them many tears

When I say I love you
please know that this is true
It was short and sweet but genuine
I'm so thankful to have met you

Patient Progression

I hate to feel
that I'm left in this place
So lost
so lonely
so bent out of shape

To open up your heart
and pour all that you have
into another soul
'till they close out the tab

The thirst it still lingers
how it burns at my throat
The yearning won't pass
my tears
I feel

~choked~

Karissa Strain

My breath
it comes fast
I just can't seem to catch
The thoughts
they play on
like a motion picture sketch
It hurts
It's fierce
like a thousand sharp knives
Cut deep
and they're twisting
My hope
how it
dies

The bubbles start rising, I swallow them down

This is not right, not what I wanted now

Karissa Strain

I'll say goodbye
but I hope it's not forever
Won't forget
about us
or this heart wrench
endeavor

I'll say goodbye
but please don't be forever
Don't forget
about us
fill my heart
make it better

Melancholy Musings of a Shameless Romantic

I hate the way
it makes me cry
every time I have to say
goodbye
I hate the way
you bring me to tears
I wanna keep you in my life
through all

~my years~

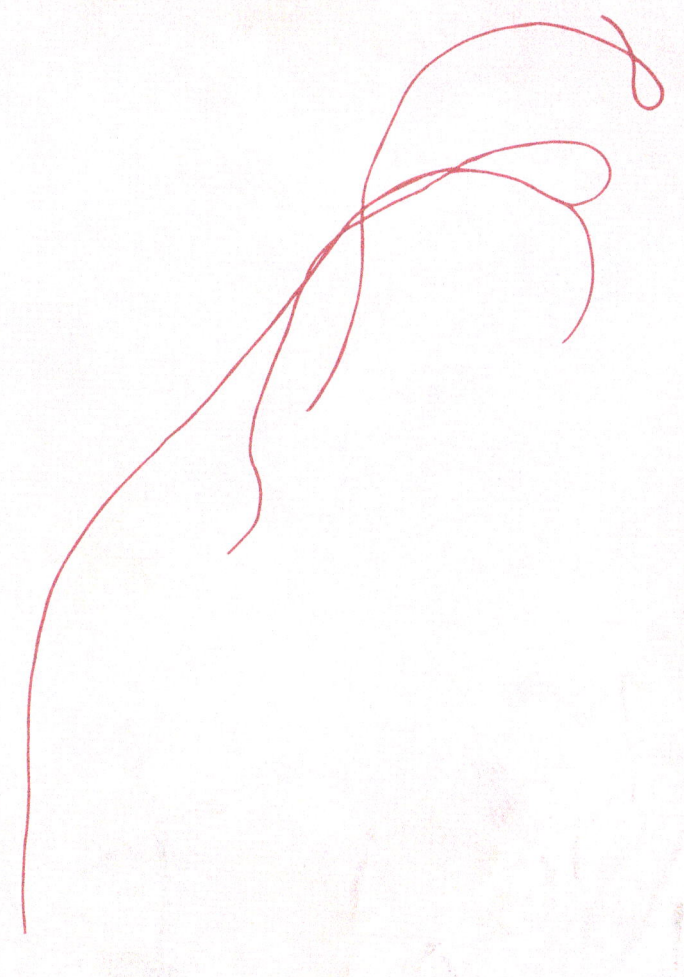

Feigning Fragilities

Now I know
it's plain to see
Failed fate was written in the stars for me
You let me down
I'll say goodbye
You beg
and I'll give it
just one more try

I'm still not sure
why I'm surprised
We've been here before must be a thousand times
You cross your heart
and I'll hope to die
The most
venomous apple
that ever caught my eye

I'd like to say
you can't catch me off guard
But I'm never prepared when you play this card
You drop the bomb
and I turn to shrapnel
I've never
known a love
so fragile

Shards of glass
slip from my eyes
A red river flows out from my insides
I said never again
would you make me cry
But you've taken
every ounce left of
my pride

It was just like the movies
It hit me with that
long pause
It hit me with that
silent read

This is just what you do to me
Your shock waves rip right through me
You take over
and I

~lose me~

Karissa Strain

I can't help
that I feel forgotten
A one-sided love
leaves a heart
that is longing
Never knowing if it's left or remains
You've got to give me something
help me

~keep the faith~

I'm still here
nothings changed
My loves unfaltering
you make my heart beat the same
So baby just tell me
are you in this game
Make up your mind boy
save us both

~the pain~

Karissa Strain

Do I give up
Do I go
Do I stay

Is it safe to let my heart show

Do I give up
Do I go
Do I stay

Don't want to guess, I've just got to know

THE LACONIC

Karissa Strain

I'm not much of a fighter
but I'd fight for you
Baby is our love true
Would you fight for me too

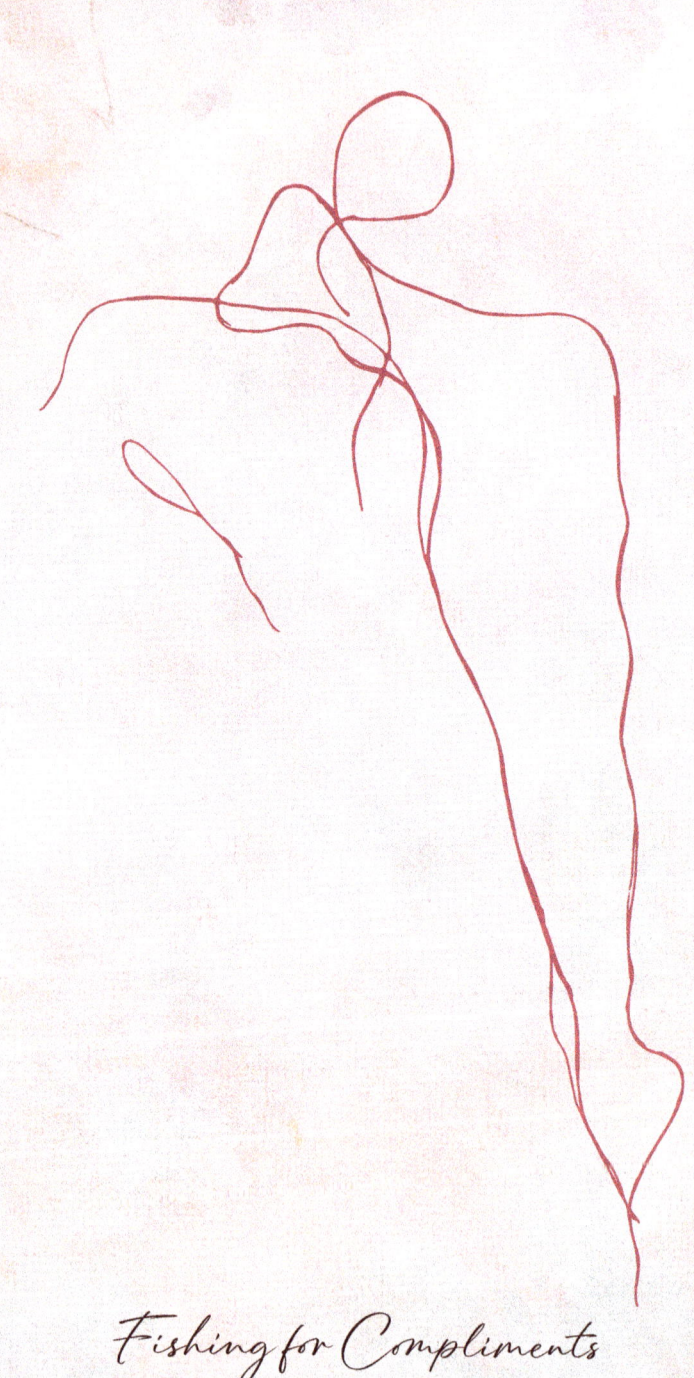

Fishing for Compliments

Karissa Strain

No one calms me in the quiet
quite like you do

I sing my soul into every word of the songs I write for him
I have to put them somewhere
It would be torturous to keep them to myself

Karissa Strain

Thoughts of you
consume me
You commandeer my mind
You move me

Raindrops
like the lips of a lover
Awakening the skin
Quaking the soul within

Karissa Strain

Wipe it all away
Lay it all to rest
Until your heart finds
It's forever
guest

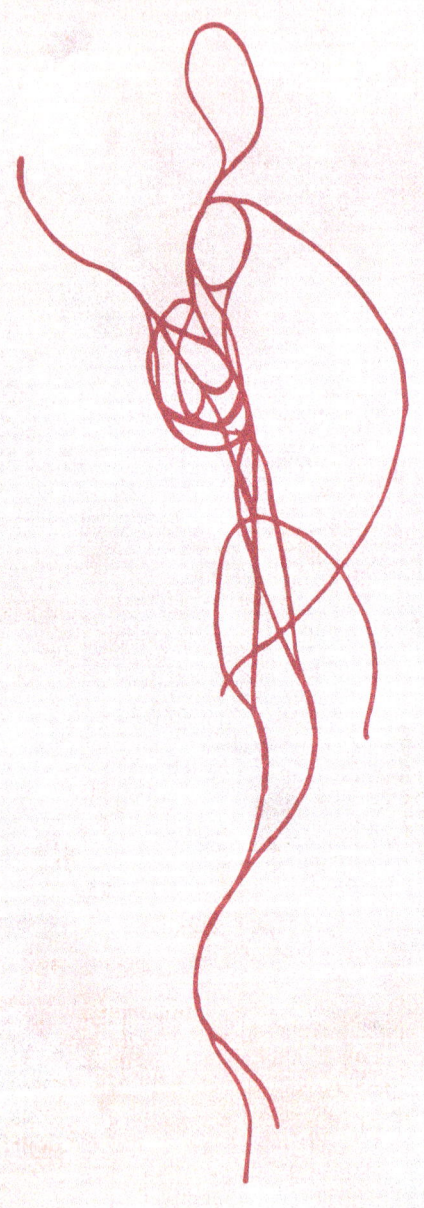

Rebirth

Ladies,

It's kind to care
to want to lend a hand
But we also simply
must understand…

>	We can't sacrifice who we are or what we want
>			in order to push someone else
>					to find out who they
>							"potentially"
>							could be

Melancholy Musings of a Shameless Romantic

I wish you would tell me everything
Everything you thought
Everything you felt
When you processed what I meant to you
So many things left undealt

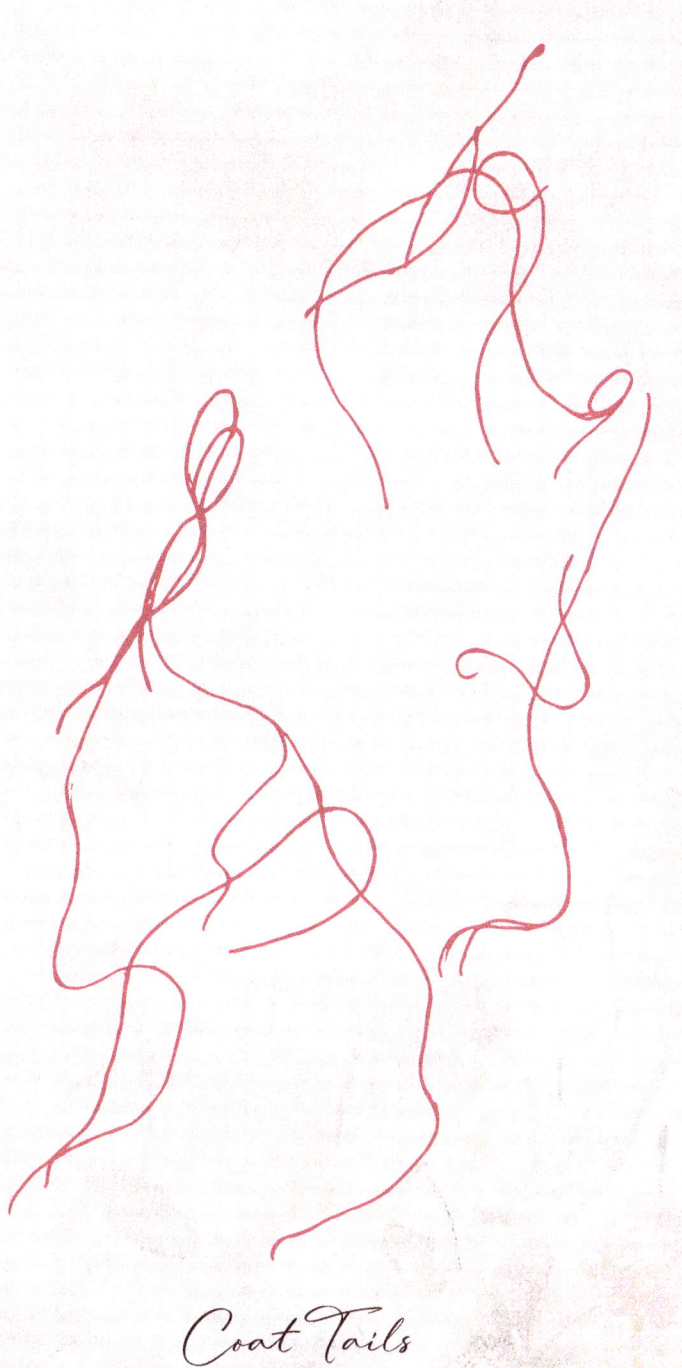

Melancholy Musings of a Shameless Romantic

If I saw you
by chance
just once more

...I would never be able
                 to
                  d
                   r
                    a
                     g
                      myself
                              away from you...

Karissa Strain

My words are like feral animals
They can only lie dormant for so long
before they thrash and gnaw to get out

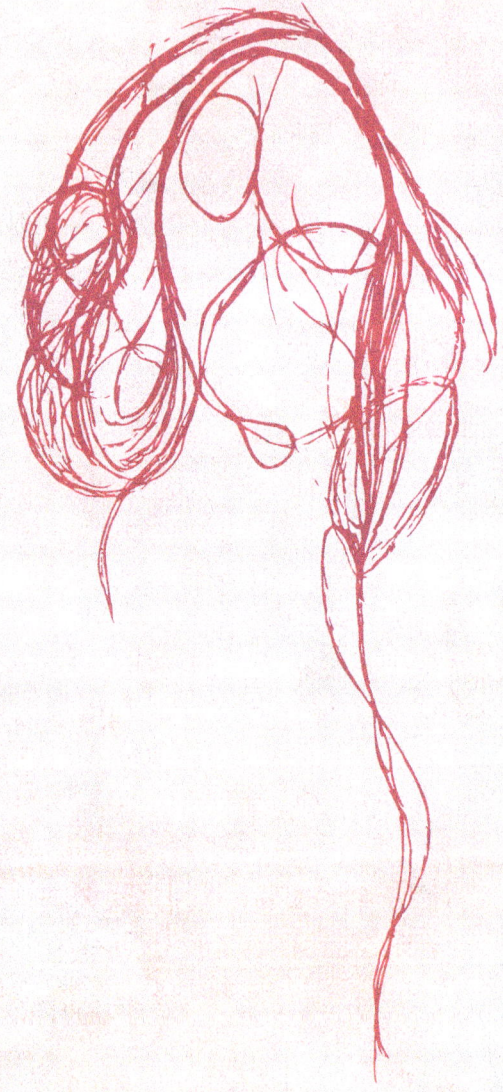

Medusa's Dog

Karissa Strain

I have so many things I want to say to you
So many things I want to ask you
But also I don't want either of us to say a word
Because more than that
More than anything
I just want to feel your arms around me again

Time spent with you
always seems too good to be true
The moments we share
are far too few
But I could never let that
make me feel blue
Because I know we'll find a way
to see each other again soon

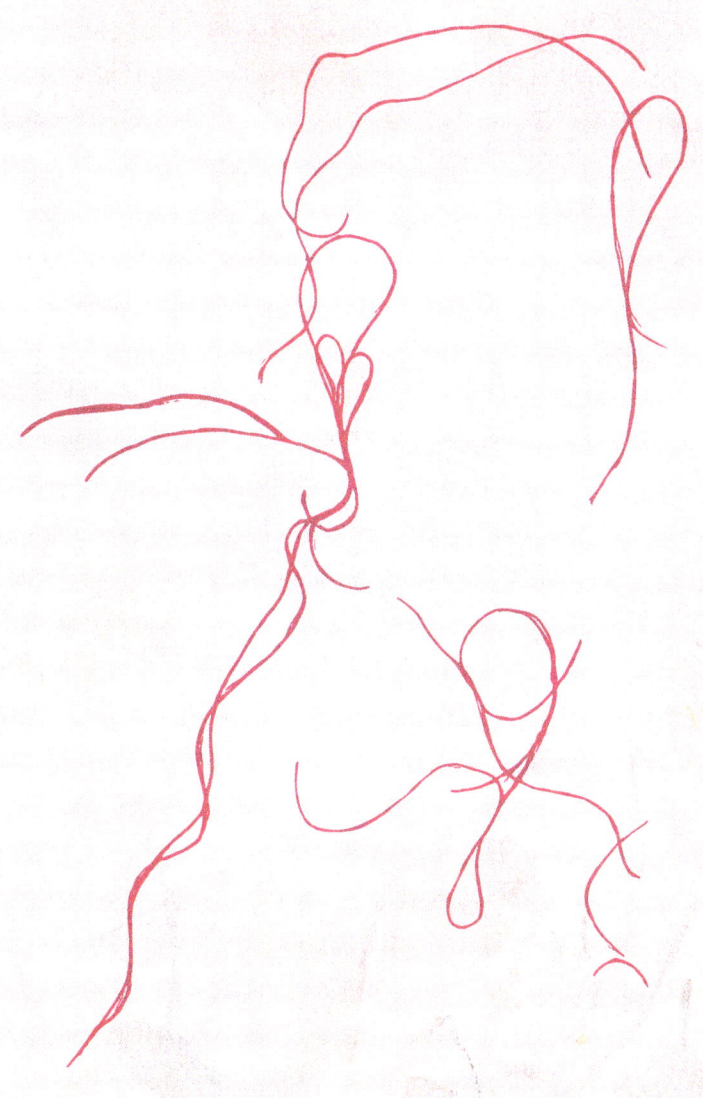

Mother of Dreamers

No matter
where I am
when I'm
with you

~I'm home~

Karissa Strain

We stayed up late
to talk about

      the human race
        and human love
          and all the things

~we're made up of~

Emotional turmoil will make you gain weight
I know this because I was my heaviest
when I was with you
Once we broke up it's like it melted away
I washed it off of me
along with your bullshit

Karissa Strain

I can't do everything.

I can see art in all things
I can hear music in all sounds
I can feel love in all people
I can choose laughter in all lulls
I can know wisdom in all words
I can find light in all darkness

That I can.

We are amazing women
Who deserve amazing men
We just haven't found the man
Willing to rise to the occasion
To be the King to our Queen

~don't forget that~

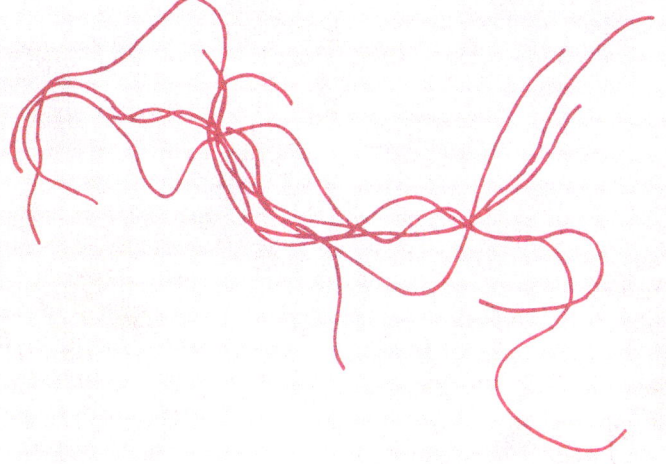

Stream-lined

Melancholy Musings of a Shameless Romantic

I want a rainy day love
the kind that falls gently
Igniting the skin
like a thousand kisses
from the burning lips of a lover

Karissa Strain

I want
An amazing
Magical
Life
I fight
Hard for it
No plans
To sacrifice

Melancholy Musings of a Shameless Romantic

In the deep blue
of the night sky
I found love
it was in your eyes
I was chasing
Always waiting
Until you showed up
now will you hold me tight

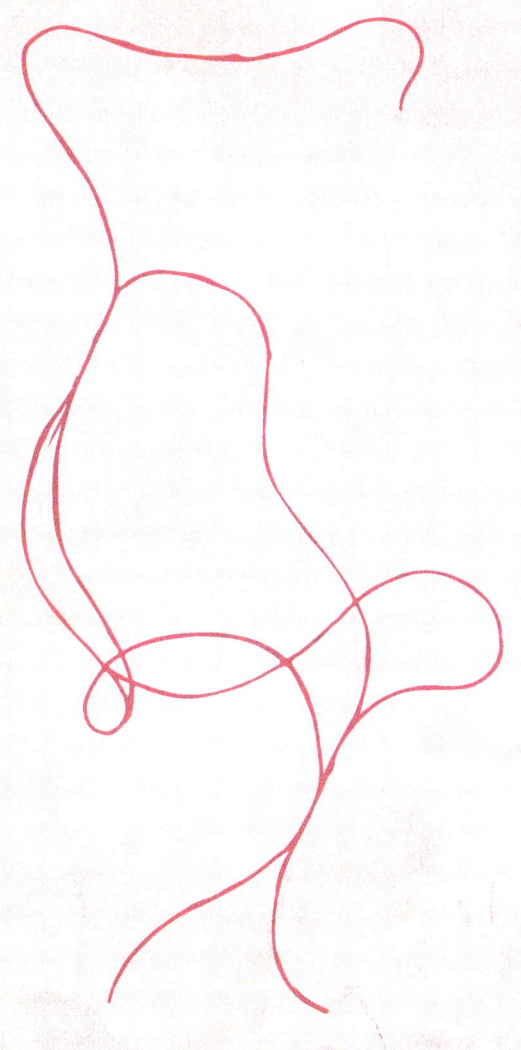

Baggage to Claim

I lied when I said I loved you
It wasn't contrived
I just didn't know what love was
until I met the man I love now

Karissa Strain

I'm taking a break.

But I won't let it break me.

Melancholy Musings of a Shameless Romantic

I'll never be a diamond love
I like it rough around the edges
Baby, be my mountain man
We'll be betting with no hedges

Karissa Strain

Something about you
makes me feel like I could
completely open myself up
and get lost in you

...but at the same time
be my most found

Don't let any man
knock your goddess
down a few pegs
just to join him
on an even
playing field

~find a new teammate~

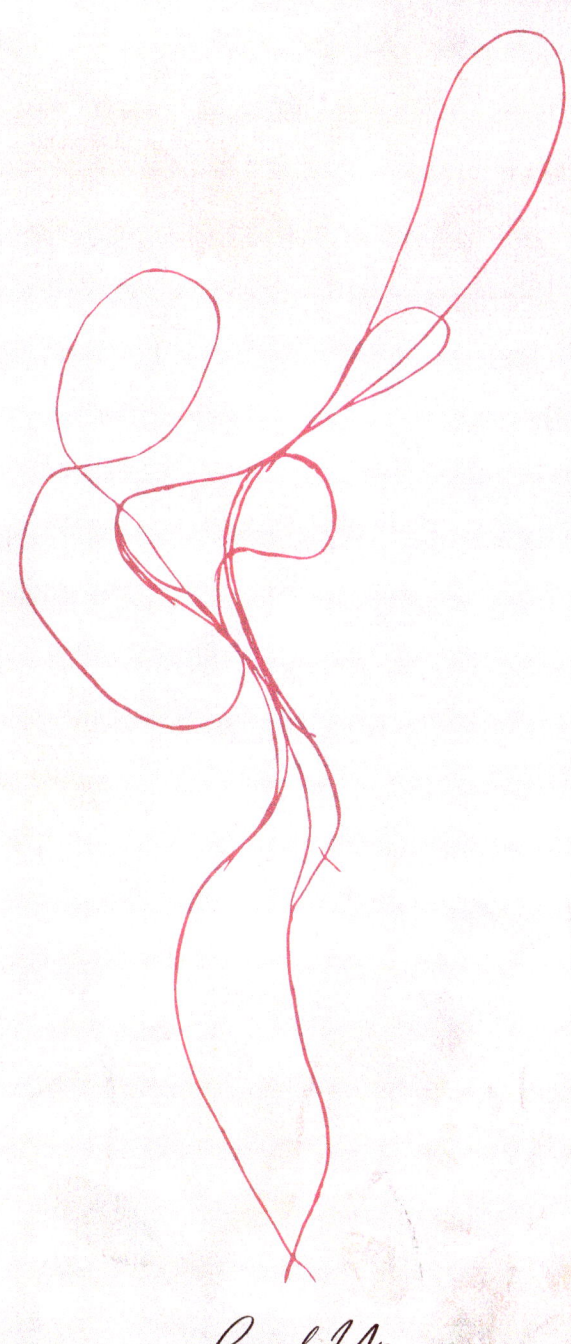

The Girl.

The Woman.

The Goddess.

Karissa Strain

Missing you is my most
   magisterial muse

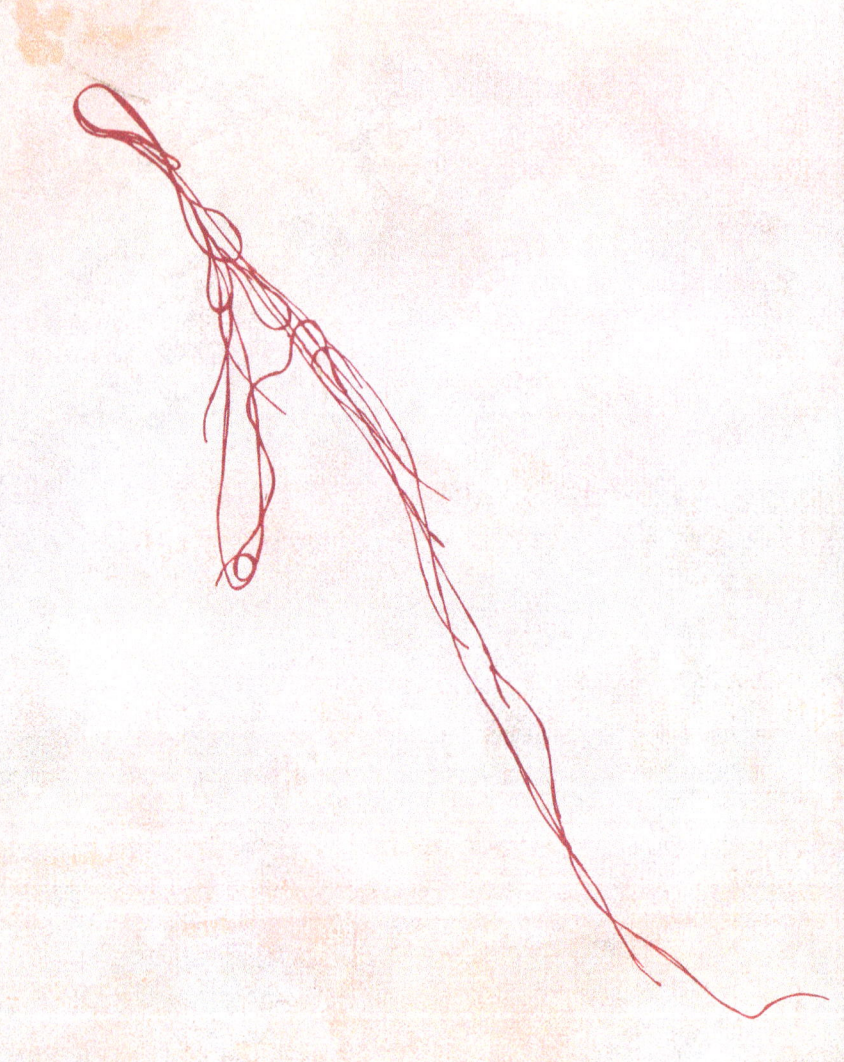

Dripping With Pride

Karissa Strain

Our words are one of our most powerful assets
I respect them
I don't give or take of them lightly

I fear that your words
are beginning to feel weightless to me

Sometimes you cry because the person you love has hurt you
Sometimes you cry because you can't be with the person you love
I'm not sure either should be indulged

...If only love never made you cry

Karissa Strain

I'm
changing
you're
pulling
on
my
heart
strings

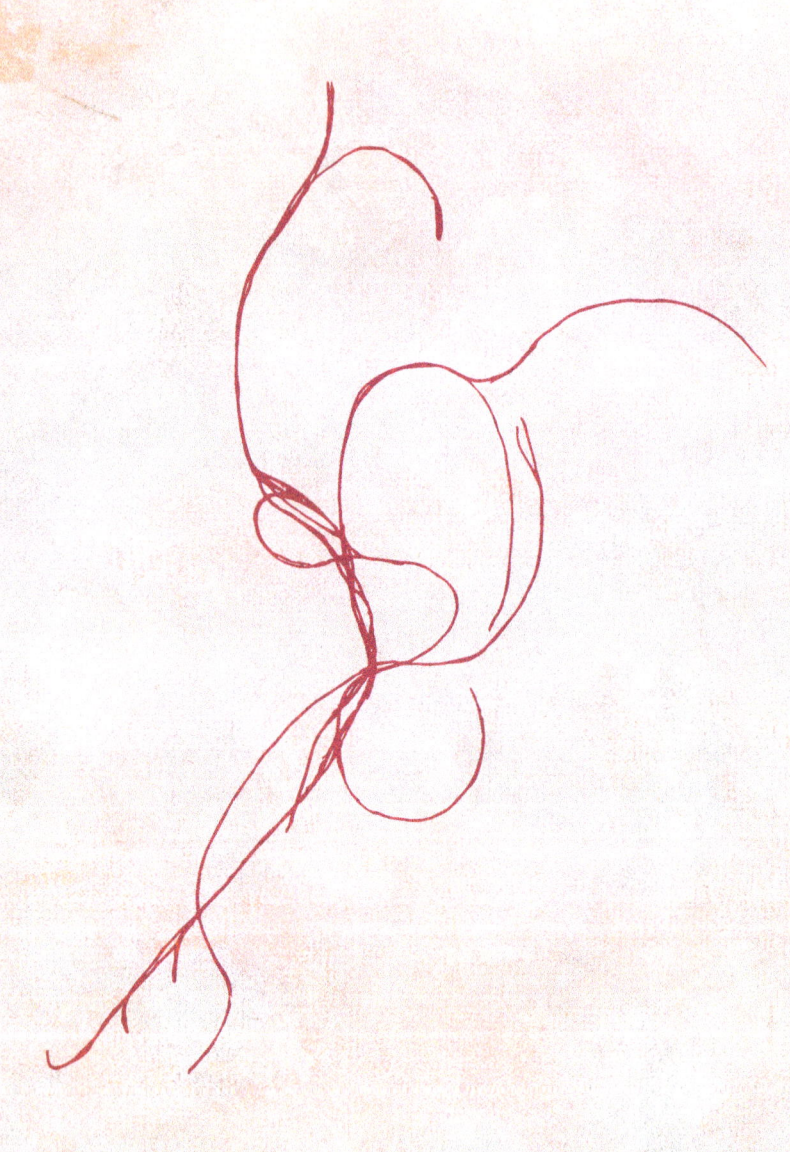

Blossom

Karissa Strain

Rainy day love
washes over me like the ocean
cleansing as the tide

Igniting feeling on my skin
like a thousand kisses
warm, soft and kind

Melancholy Musings of a Shameless Romantic

Let's undo all the damage
our past hurts have done
Let me shine for you
I want to be your sun

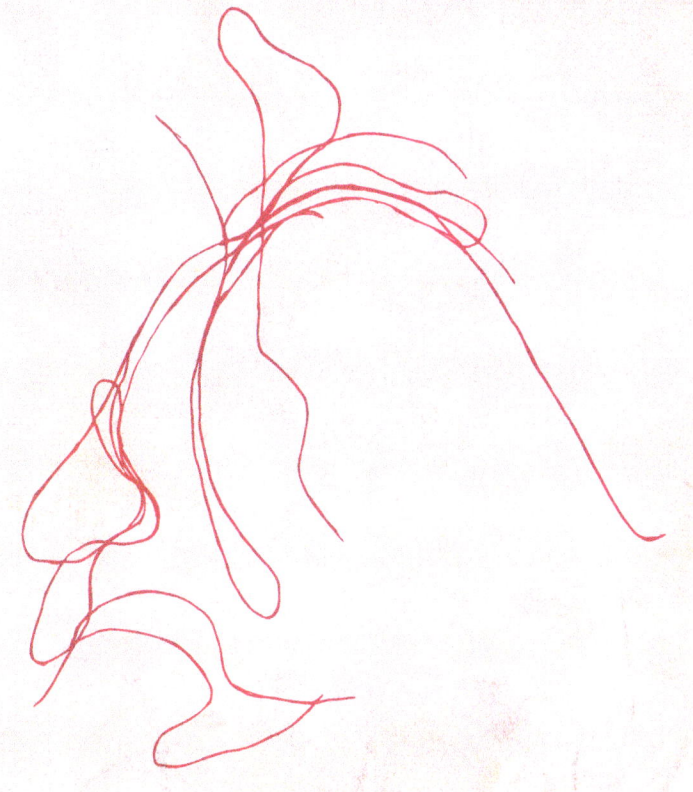

Free Falling

I'm forever.

Forever a fool.

Forever a fool for you.

Forever.

Karissa Strain

We're celestial bodies
in synchronous rotation
I'll be locked to your sky
through all of our successions

Melancholy Musings of a Shameless Romantic

You're my easy rain
The wind blew you in
to wash my cares away
as you land upon my skin

I WILL...

I will choose me

I will be passionate

I will be positive

I will be adventurous

I will be unafraid

I will be daring

I will work hard

I will be responsible

I will respect my body

I will be healthy

I will be working

I will be creative

I will sing

I will paint

I will drive

I will dance

I will be sunshine

I will be love

I will learn

I will grow

I will be grateful

I will be kind

I will be laughter

I will be light

I will be free

I will cherish

I will appreciate

I will take time

I will be patient

I will rest

I will sweat

I will be strong

I will be silent

I will be heard

I will be heart

I will be adored

I will be successful

I will be respected

I will feel

I will be a fool

I will be a dreamer

I will be a fighter

I will be a lover

I will be a friend

I will be calm

I will be change

...I will be ME

I WILL BE!

About the Author

I don't write poetry.
Poetry writes me.
It writes my mood, my actions, my thoughts and my feelings.
It writes my questions, my muses, my curiosities
and my disappointments.
It writes my triumphs, my travails, my loves as well as my losses.
For as long as I can remember I have been a very sensitive
and emotional person. I often thought, and through the early
years of my adulthood I was often told (mostly by
my romantic partners) that my sensitivities were a shortcoming.
I was too emotional.
I was too soft.
It made me weak, and vulnerable and I needed to work harder
to curb those natural inclinations.
I foolishly believed that for a while, until I learned that
my ability to feel deeply and channel those sensitivities
is actually one of my biggest strengths.
My words became my therapy.
My words became my shield from others scorns.
My words became my biggest pride and my constant supporter.
My words became my most fulfilling artistic outlet.
My words became my solace.

For whatever I may lack in life
I will always covet the courage of my words.